A LITTLE BOOK OF

CRICKET

ALLSORTED.

This edition first published in Great Britain in 2024
by Allsorted Ltd, WD19 4BG, U.K.

The facts and statistics in this book are correct up to the end of the 2023/24 season. The data comes from publicly available sources and is presented as correct as far as our knowledge allows. The opinions in this book are personal and individual and are not affiliated to the football club in any way. Any views or opinions represented in this book are personal and belong solely to the book author and do not represent those of people, institutions or organisations that the football club or publisher may or may not be associated with in professional or personal capacity, unless explicitly stated. Any views or opinions are not intended to malign any religious, ethnic group, club, organisation, company or individual.

All rights reserved. No part of this work may be reproduced in any form or by any means, electronic or mechanical, including photocopying, recording or by any information storage and retrieval system, without the prior written permission of the publisher.

© Susanna Geoghegan Gift Publishing
Author: Magnus Allan
Cover design: Milestone Creative
Contents design: Bag of Badgers Ltd
Illustrations: Ludovic Sallé

ISBN: 978-1-915902-58-0

Printed in China

• A LITTLE BOOK OF CRICKET •

 # CONTENTS

Contents	Stand and delivery 42	Sir Alastair Cook 110
Introduction 5	Brief history of bowling 44	Cricket and the weather 112
The first rules of cricket club 8	Jacques Kallis 50	Imran Khan 116
World test wicket-takers 10	Fielding positions 52	What even is cow corner? 118
The umpire's first strike 13	M.S. Dhoni 72	Ben Stokes 120
James Anderson 14	The MCC steps up to the crease 74	Six balls to an over 122
Historic Hambledon 16	Spin bowlers 76	Fred Trueman 130
Wholesome fun on dry land 19	Wakey wakey, egg and bakey 79	Fast bowlers 133
The Hambledon salon 20	Women's cricket 81	World test centuries 136
World test run-makers 23	Sophie Ecclestone 84	Andrew Flintoff 138
A victim of its own success 25	World test catchers 86	The chirping, bantering, sledging 140
The bat 26	Wickets – so good 88	Sir Vivian Richards 144
W.G. Grace 32	What the format? 90	Cricket pads 146
The passage of history 35	The covers 94	Wicketkeepers 148
Sir Richard Hadlee 36	Balls 96	Alan Knott 152
Why is a cricket pitch ...? 38	Shane Warne 100	Cricket at the Olympics 154
Sir Ian Botham 40	The Ashes of history 103	Tail-enders 156
	Denis Compton 104	Stuart Broad 158
	How tho Achoc came to be 107	

> "Cricket is not just a sport; it's a way of life."

Professional cricketer Eoin Morgan makes an astute observation.

★ INTRODUCTION ★

The bottom line is that cricket is old. Really old. Older than television. Older than the first French Revolution. Older than the Rolling Stones. It's been a central fixture of summer entertainment in some parts of England since at least the 16th century.

It's the quintessential summer game: a game of patience where, even to the initiated, nothing seems to be happening for long periods of time — and then it's all over in a bewildering clutch of seconds. The truth is that while it looks like nothing's happening, there are a hundred little changes being made — to the bowlers' deliveries, to the fielders' positions, to the batters' stance — with each having a subtle influence on what could be about to happen.

The sport we know today started to coalesce in the mid-18th century, but there were certainly games of what you could call proto-cricket being played before then. We know this because of things like court records that mention the game.

For example, there's a legal case in 1597 about the use of a parcel of land in Surrey that mentions that cricket had been played there since at least 1550. More darkly, in 1624, coroners recorded the death of one Jasper Vinall. He was playing in a match in Sussex when he went in to make a catch, presumably fairly close to the batter. Unfortunately, the batter, Edward Tye, didn't fancy being caught and given out so he stepped up to take a second strike at the ball in the air, connecting with Vinall's head instead. He died 13 days later.

There was nothing in the rules at the time to stop a batter taking a second hit, so a second person, Henry Brand, is recorded as being killed in similar circumstances in 1647. It seems likely that these incidents were the reason why one of the first sets of official cricket rules in 1744 prohibited batters taking second hits.

Either way, they are proof that a game called cricket was being played in the south of England well before the dawn of the modern era.

Cricket has changed a bit in the ensuing years, but perhaps not by as much as you'd expect. From what historians can tell, the game being played on the South Downs used a curved bat – a bit like a hockey stick – because balls used to be bowled along the ground (see page 44). It gradually morphed into the paddle-like shape we might recognise today in the late 18th century, after the curious case of the monster bat (see page 26).

There is data and information about matches and players stretching back for a couple of hundred years, but it's patchy. The game has also changed in subtle ways over the last few years, with new formats changing both what's possible and what's expected. What has been consistent throughout, though, is that cricket has thrown up some amazing characters and some fascinating stories down the years.

★ THE FIRST RULES OF ★ CRICKET CLUB

Cricket's first recorded written rules were penned in 1727 by Alan Brodrick, the second Viscount Midleton, and his chum Charles Lennox, the second Duke of Richmond. From such humble roots did mighty modern cricket grow ...

Rules are likely to have existed prior to this, but there would probably have been local variations. Every house has slightly different rules for Uno, so why should cricket be any different? A standardised set of rules was needed for a fairly simple reason: Brodrick and Lennox used to arrange games of cricket, and the Articles of Agreement saved them from having to spend an hour or so before each match discussing how they were going to play.

Sixteen rules were laid out in the Articles of Agreement, including a specified 23 yards between the wickets, which is pretty close to the 22-yard distance still used nearly 300 years later. There are those who suggest that the 23-yard distance written down in the articles could be an error given that the 22-yard chain (see page 38) was a standard unit of measurement at the time.

"One could not define what cricket was, as one could not define a gentleman, but one knew it, as one knew a gentleman when one met a gentleman,"

claimed Stanley Baldwin, Prime Minister of the United Kingdom, in 1929. He'd never heard of the case of the monster bat, which quite clearly just wasn't cricket.

Player	Years	Wkts
Dale Steyn (SA)	2004–2019	439
Ravichandran Ashwin (IND)	2011–2024	516
Courtney Walsh (WI)	1984–2001	519
Nathan Lyon (AUS)	2011–2024	530
Glenn McGrath (AUS)	1993–2007	563
Stuart Broad (ENG)	2007–2023	604
Anil Kumble (IND)	1990–2008	619
James Anderson (ENG)	2003–2024	704
Shane Warne (AUS)	1992–2007	708
Muthiah Muralidaran (ICC/SL)	1992–2010	800

· A LITTLE BOOK OF CRICKET ·

★ WORLD TEST WICKET-TAKERS ★

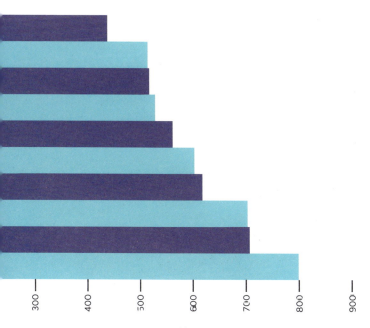

> "The real character of a player is tested in tough situations on the cricket field."

Australia's Ricky Ponting was rarely found wanting.

★ THE UMPIRE'S FIRST STRIKE ★

Brodrick and Lennox were also keen to ensure that the umpire's word was final, with the 11th article stating:

> *that there shall be one Umpire of each side; & that if any of the Gamesters* [players] *shall speak or give of their opinion, on any Point of the Game, they are to be turned out, & Voided in the Match; this not to extend to the Duke of Richmond & Mr. Brodrick.*

This suggests two things. Firstly, you are only allowed an opinion if you are a mid-ranking member, or higher, of the British aristocracy. What's the point in setting the rules – and bankrolling the game – if you are not allowed to challenge umpires?

Secondly, it sounds like there might have been complaints about umpires' decisions in the past, and so Brodrick and Lennox wanted to avoid controversy. It is interesting to note that respect for umpires' decisions was built into the earliest forms of the modern game.

· A LITTLE BOOK OF CRICKET ·

★ JAMES ANDERSON ★
(ENGLAND)

Jimmy Anderson is England's leading Test wicket-taker. With more than 700 Test wickets to his name, he's the third highest Test wicket-taker in the history of world cricket. He's taken 32 five-wicket hauls in his 187 Tests, going on to take 10 wickets on three occasions. Basically, he's a bowling machine.

Anderson made his One Day International (ODI) debut before he'd earned his first County cap. He took his first five-for in his Test debut against Zimbabwe in 2003, embellishing the feat by taking all five wickets in a single innings. He took a bit of time to become a fixture of the England team, but in the process he turned himself into one of the most voracious wicket-takers that the game has seen. He was at the heart of the England team that won three consecutive Ashes series between 2009 and 2013, the first time that had been achieved since 1977–1981.

Someday the Barmy Army's trumpet will stop playing his tune, and English cricket will be significantly diminished, but there's no doubt he's inspired plenty of future heroes.

Anderson's retirement at the start of the 2024 Test season left England with a heavy heart and potentially a big gap in their attack. He spent the best part of two decades at the centre of the England team and cemented himself into position as one of England's greatest sportspeople.

HISTORIC HAMBLEDON

Cricket's ancestral home is not actually the Marylebone Cricket Club (MCC), the Oval, Edgbaston or any of the famous first-class English pitches. The so-called 'cradle of cricket' is the sleepy Hampshire hamlet of Hambledon, home to around 1,000 people and boasting a primary school that's been recently rated as 'Outstanding' by Ofsted, the government department that is supposed to be responsible for that sort of thing in England. (Northern Ireland, Scotland and Wales have their own things going on.) It's technically a village but 'Hampshire hamlet of Hambledon' had a nice ring to it.

Nestled in the comforting chalklands of the South Downs National Park, it's the sort of place where people use the word 'splendid' without irony. If you settle down for a pint in one of its two charming pubs, you can be certain that someone in a pair of red chinos will saunter past within five minutes, a black Labrador vaguely at their heel ... And look, over there in the car park, isn't that Chief Inspector Barnaby and one of his interchangeable sidekicks? They're a bit far south, but they look right at home. It's that sort of a place.

> "You can't be a good cricketer without being a good person off the field,"

says India's Sunil Gavaskar, and it would be nice to believe that he's right.

"**Cricket is a game that teaches you patience, perseverance, and the value of teamwork,**"

says Brian Lara of the West Indies. Was it patience or impatience that made him the fastest batter to score 10,000 (alongside Sachin Tendulkar) and 11,000 Test runs, in terms of number of innings?

★ WHOLESOME FUN ON DRY LAND ★

Urban snobbery aside, in around 1750, the Hambledon Cricket Club was formed and started to put together cricket matches. Why Hambledon? Aside from it being quintessentially English and very pretty, it was also relatively convenient for Portsmouth, and the whole set-up seems to have been built around a group of naval officers who wanted something wholesome to do with their shore-leave. A local innkeeper spotted an opportunity and started hosting said gentlemen, offering them a table, some chairs and some light refreshments so they had a base from which to play. At some point, the inn was renamed from 'the Hutt' to 'the Bat & Ball'.

Cricket at Hambledon was mainly an excuse to bring people together for a feast and quietly place a wager or two on the outcome of a match. But the Hambledon team became pretty good, starting the process of turning cricket from a knockabout into something more like an art. By the mid-1770s, the Hambledon club were taking on all-England teams and winning.

★ THE HAMBLEDON SALON ★

Part of the reason why the team became so good was that many of the players were professionals, paid to play cricket but also organise and set up the matches (mostly so the gentlemen could indulge in some serious roistering while the match went on – huzzah!). In a weird way, this baked professionalism into cricket from its very earliest days, meaning that it could sidestep the tensions that some other sports suffered in the mid-19th century as they grappled with the rights and wrongs of paying players.

According to many historical records, crowds were flocking to watch Hambledon play, and the club itself was doing very nicely indeed from the proceeds of the wagers being put on matches. It's not too much of a surprise, therefore, that its success accelerated the development of formal cricket in other parts of the country, too.

> **"Ninety per cent of cricket is played in the mind,"**
>
> observed New Zealand's Richard Hadlee. Imagine what he would have achieved if he'd put 15 per cent of his effort onto the field.

Player	Years	Runs
Joe Root (ENG)	2012–2024	11,736
Mahela Jayawardene (SL)	1997–2014	11,814
Shivnarine Chanderpaul (WI)	1994–2015	11,867
Brian Lara (ICC/WI)	1990–2006	11,953
Kumar Sangakkara (SL)	2000–2015	12,400
Alastair Cook (ENG)	2006–2018	12,472
Rahul Dravid (ICC/IND)	1996–2012	13,288
Jacques Kallis (ICC/SA)	1995–2013	13,289
Ricky Ponting (AUS)	1995–2012	13,378
Sachin Tendulkar (IND)	1989–2013	15,921

WORLD TEST RUN-MAKERS

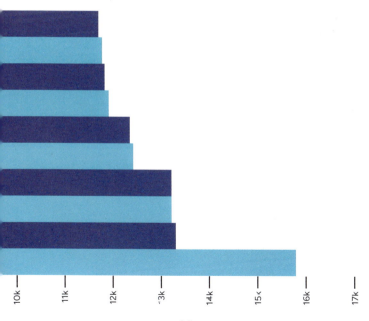

> "What I do is creak out to the square and hope to plonk a little timber on the ball,"

actor and cricket aficionado Peter O'Toole reflects on his approach to the game.

A VICTIM OF ITS OWN SUCCESS

Several of the gentlemen that had enjoyed the Hampshire hospitality regularly came down from London. While they presumably very much enjoyed their trips down to the south, they figured that they could have as much fun closer to town without the faff of what would then have been a day's travel by stagecoach.

By the late 1880s, cricket clubs were forming in London, the Hambledon club dwindled, the caravan moved on and by 1796 it returned to being pretty much a village cricket club after three decades at the heart of the cricketing universe.

The interesting thing about Hambledon is that some of the paper trail of what went on there is very well preserved, offering quite detailed insights into cricket as it started down the road to the modern game. The game was being played elsewhere, but Hambledon appears to be where it all started coming together.

 THE BAT

Cricket is an eternal battle between batting and fielding, which probably says something exceptionally profound about humanity's perception of its place in the universe. But it is also a sport that people have been quick to place wagers on – and when there are wagers, there are sometimes unscrupulous people who will do anything to get an advantage.

As a result, rules have had to be made – and then refined – to ensure that there is a level playing field between the two sides.

The curious case of the monster bat

Take, for example, the notorious day in 1771 when the batsman representing Chertsey, thought to be Thomas 'Daddy' White, strode out to defend his wicket against the increasingly renowned Hambledon bowling attack. There were two Whites on the pitch that day, hence the slight uncertainty whether it was Daddy White or the alternative who appears, for some reason, to have been called Shock White (things would be much neater if he had been known as 'Son').

Either way, as White emerged from the pavilion and made his way to the crease, he unveiled what can only be described as a fiendishly cunning plan to protect his wicket: a bat that was fully as wide as the stumps.

At the time there no rules to stop White doing this, but a member of the Hambledon team is said to have snatched the offending bat away from him and stomped off to find a carpenter to shave it down to size. A few days later, the Hambledon organising committee, who were the guardians of cricket's thin – but rapidly expanding – rulebook at the time, added a new law: bats should be no wider than four-and-a-quarter inches (which is 10.8 cm in real money).

They are also said to have produced the first metal gauge so that umpires could confirm that bats measured up. The 10.8 cm width has remained in place ever since. Wide enough to offer some, but not complete, protection for the wicket, which is set at 22.86 cm (9 inches) wide.

It didn't stop there, though ...

Cricket bats have to do four things.

1. They have to be able to connect and transfer as much energy as possible to the ball as it comes towards the batter.

2. They have to be solid enough to withstand being hit repeatedly by said ball moving at speed.

3. They need to be supple enough to give a batter the finesse they are looking for in the strokes.

4. They also need to be light enough to be carried and run with for – what all batters hope will be – a long day at the crease.

English willow has tended to be seen as the best type of wood for the job for the majority of the last 250 years, although different woods are being tried all the time.

The shape of the bat has been fairly consistent throughout, but special mention should go to the Scoop, which took the world of 1970s and 1980s cricket by storm. The Scoop had thicker edges, giving the bat a wider sweet spot – the point that gives the best acceleration of the ball with the least vibration for the batter. However, to reduce the weight, the manufacturers scooped out the ridge down the back of the bat's blade. The design was recently reintroduced and, by all accounts, is still selling well.

ComBat and Mongoose bats

There have been other attempts to make changes. The aluminium ComBat (see what they did there?) was actively discouraged after complaints that the aluminium was damaging the ball. The Mongoose turned up just in time for the rise of the aggressive Twenty20 (T20) form of the game in the early 2000s and looked like it might fare a little better. It was all handle and relatively little bat, which gave it a decent-sized sweet spot that was well suited to slugging the ball around the pitch.

Bowlers fairly quickly decoded its flaw, though: less blade meant less protection for the batter, so a couple of brusque bouncers finding their way over the body of the bat and into the leg had batters reaching back into their kit bags to reinstate the Old Faithful fairly quickly.

Evolution never stops ... There has been a debate about the depth of the willow on some modern bats because modern drying and pressing techniques have enhanced the wood so they are lighter and stronger, potentially giving batters an unfair advantage. After much stroking of chins, in 2017 the international cricket authorities issued new restrictions on the depth of a bat: 10.8 cm width, 6.7 cm depth and with edges of 4.0 cm.

It may be in the future that cricketers will have to get used to the glorious sound of leather on bamboo heralding the arrival of summer; for now, though, the cricket bat is what it has mostly always been: a solid lump of willow that brings the fun. As of 2017, though, it's a more closely defined solid lump of willow.

> "I'm jealous of my parents; I'll never have a kid as cool as theirs."

Someday Chris Gayle's daughter will read that comment.

· A LITTLE BOOK OF CRICKET ·

★ W.G. GRACE ★
(ENGLAND)

If you say the words 'English cricket' to most people, one of the first things that will flash through their mind is the image of a large Victorian bloke with a mahoosive beard, a cricket bat in hand and a small cap perched on top of his head. Same way that if you mention kings of England; everyone always gets that image of Henry VIII, arms akimbo and feet placed wide in history's first power pose.

There's a simple reason for this: Grace was a mainstay of the English Test team for two decades, dominated the sport for the best part of 35 years, and is widely regarded as the player who popularised the modern game.

While cricket tends to have particularly good records of its 19th-century exploits (and would probably have had fairly good records of its 18th-century exploits if the pavilion at Lords, where the paperwork was kept, hadn't gone up in smoke in 1825), it's still difficult to compare them with what is being achieved today. There is also some suggestion that Grace's larger-than-life character and extensive influence in the game tended to encourage his version of events to be the one documented rather than the one that everyone else might have thought they had seen. Either way, he is recorded as making more than 54,000 first-class runs and taken around 2,800 wickets, which is not small beer.

Grace remained an amateur throughout his career, nominally earning a crust as a doctor but supplementing his wage through a variety of expense claims that most modern finance departments would smirk at shortly before writing a snotty email to the submitter's line manager and hitting the big red reject button.

He was what we, today, would call a complex character, but there's little doubt that he was absolutely committed to cricket and was pivotal in the sport's development.

> During an otherwise unremarkable 1898 match between Gloucestershire and Sussex, W.G. Grace declared innings whilst batting – on a personal tally of 93. It transpired he had every score from 0-99 – except 93. His son was yet to bat …

★ THE PASSAGE OF HISTORY ★

While Hambledon has a fair claim to have been the epicentre of cricket's modernisation, there was a lively cricketing culture developing throughout the south-east of England during the 18th century.

What evolved into the MCC appears to have started out on White Conduit Fields in rural Islington. Cricket had been being played there since at least 1718, which we know because there are court records of two teams that got into a legal tussle about the terms of a wager that they had been playing for. The world has turned a few times since those days, but it's fascinating that reports in 18th-century local newspapers tend to talk about which side won the wager rather than which side won the match.

By 1782, the White Conduit Club had been formed, bringing together several well-funded, London-based cricket enthusiasts. They organised games and hired professional cricketers to play them while they got on with the serious business of placing bets against the outcome of the match. Among the notables running the club was the imaginatively named Charles Lennox, who went on to become the fourth Duke of Richmond and was, incidentally, the grandson of Charles Lennox, second Duke of Richmond.

· A LITTLE BOOK OF CRICKET ·

★ SIR RICHARD HADLEE ★
(NEW ZEALAND)

Walter Hadlee captained the highly-regarded New Zealand Test team that came to England on tour in 1949. He had five children, three of whom represented the Black Caps, and one of whom, Sir Richard Hadlee, went on to become one of the most celebrated cricketers of his generation.

Richard Hadlee took a wicket in his Test debut against England in 1973 and enjoyed a five-wicket haul during his Test final day of work with the ball against England 17 years later. His Test wicket total was 431, the 13th highest in cricket history. He was also handy with the bat, scoring two Test centuries and 15 half-centuries and helping New Zealand score their first Test victory against England on English soil in 1983. He topped both the batting and the bowling averages in that series.

In later life, when his father Walter was asked by cricketing almanac Wisden to name his five best cricketers of the 20th century, he included Richard on his list. No one suggested he was showing favouritism, but it's probably safe to assume that the next family dinner was a little subdued.

WHY IS A CRICKET PITCH ...?

The thing about cricket being a relatively old sport is that very few people thought to keep records of its really early days, but if you scratch the surface, certain facts can be gleaned from the evidence presented.

A full-sized cricket pitch is 20.12 metres from stump to stump and 3.05 metres from side to side. These might seem like random numbers, but if you convert them back into pre-decimal measurements, you end up with a far more wholesome 22 yards long (1 chain) by 3.33 yards (10 feet) wide.

All right, 22 yards still seems slightly arbitrary but, back in the day, 22 yards was a standard measurement for land, also known as a 'chain'. If you are interested, the chain is a tenth of a furlong, which was thought to be the average length of land that a team of oxen could plough without resting. The chain, which was literally a physical chain, also used to have 100 links in it so that people who measured stuff could look at sub-divisions. It might seem complicated but our ancestors managed to make it work – and who are we to judge?

The chain has long-since been dropped as a unit of measurement, although it still echoes back from history in things like cricket. Why hasn't cricket decimalised? Because the most logical way to do that would be to make the pitch smaller by 0.12 metres, which would mean that batters had even less time to react to a ball coming at them at speed – and nobody wants to go through an entire season listening to fast bowlers moan about the pitch being the wrong length. It's easier to leave it as a glorious anachronism, because it turns out that none of us can break the chain.

> **Indian batter Dilip Vengesarkar, known to his chums as Colonel, is the only overseas player to have scored three successive centuries on the Lord's ground, achieving his feat in 1979, 1982 and 1986. He is remembered as an exceptional proponent of the drive, but also had a sweet hook.**

· A LITTLE BOOK OF CRICKET ·

★ SIR IAN BOTHAM ★
(ENGLAND)

With three years of senior cricket under his belt, Ian Botham strode on to the stage in 1976, cricket bat in one hand, bowl of shredded wheat in the other. The lights went up and the audience held its breath. He enjoyed a meteoric rise during that long, hot summer of 1976: even if he only scored a single run in his international debut, his domestic stats were impressive.

By the time the Ashes rolled around in July 1977, Botham took two five-fors in consecutive tests, something that became a bit of a habit over his career. He has still taken the ninth-most five-wicket hauls in an innings in the history of Test cricket, and is one of only two bowlers prior to 1990 to feature in that particular top 10, alongside Richard Hadlee (see page 36).

Botham began to develop a reputation as a match winner, helping lead the England charge with both bat and ball, and by 1980 he was made captain of the Test team, although a dip in form meant that he only held the role for two years.

Having a lot of potential as a footballer, Beefy turned out for both Yeovil Town and Scunthorpe United, but felt he had more opportunities as a cricketer.

Botham has been knighted for his services to charity and cricket and sits in the House of Lords as a crossbench peer.

★ STAND AND DELIVERY ★

As London continued its urban sprawl, the fine gentlemen of the White Conduit Club could see a point where their playing fields were going to become enclosed by the growing city. There was a risk that by the dawn of the 19th century, there wouldn't be any fields between King's Cross and Islington. Imagine. To be fair, though, White Conduit Fields were just off the main road out of north London and were apparently frequented by pickpockets, highwaymen, miscreants and all manner of ne'er-do-wells, so the gentry wanted somewhere they could go out to bat and be sure that their wallet would be there when they got back. Probably because it had a betting slip in it.

So they sent Thomas Lord (mark the name, it'll be important), one of their groundsmen and a prominent bowler of the age, to find somewhere quieter where they could indulge their passion for cricket.

Lord found a good spot and, in 1787, the White Conduit Club decamped to Marylebone and started playing at what has come to be known as 'Lord's Old Ground'. The club changed its name to the 'Marylebone Cricket Club' in the process.

"I tend to think that cricket is the greatest thing that God ever created on earth – certainly greater than sex, although sex isn't too bad either."

Playwright Harold Pinter proves he was no playboy.

★ A BRIEF HISTORY OF BOWLING ★

There is, you'll be surprised to hear, a little bit of historical murk in all this – but when cricket first started out, there was none of this steaming up like a wild bull and trying to send the bales to Wales, as the kids so gleefully say. Cricket was a gentle sport, and the art of bowling was all in the wrist. Deliveries were underarm and the ball could not be released above waist height, from the sounds of things, a bit like the way balls are thrown in the game of bowls.

It wasn't until around the 1760s that cricket balls started to be pitched underarm at batters, rather than rolled at them. No one really knows how or why the change happened; it's mostly only observed in the changing drawings of the game at around that point, which start to show bowlers making deliveries from a standing position rather than a crouch.

It may be, given the bowls-like delivery and the croquet-like two wickets that were originally deployed, that cricket started out as a cousin of these two games, but it seems unlikely we will ever know.

Never let the facts get in the way ...

The transition to overarm bowling was slow and considered. Thomas Walker, who played for Hampshire at Hambledon back in the day, is said to have realised in the late 18th century that bowling with his arm away from his body meant that he could make the balls more difficult to play, but the cricketing authorities, such as they were, took a dim view of this kind of madness and it was never allowed to catch on.

This might be why the 1816 rules made roundarm bowling illegal, but the concept wouldn't go away.

There is a story that in around 1807, a Kent county bowler by the name of John Willes was getting some throw-downs (practice balls) from his sister, Christina or Christiana Willes. She was wearing a massively hooped skirt (although the fashion was all a bit *Bridgerton* at the time), and this crinoline and waggon wheel confection was allegedly getting in the way of her arm, so she decided to bowl roundarm, which opened up a whole new range of angles of attack (practice balls are always spicy between siblings). This set John Willes to thinking and he resolved to try to get roundarm accepted in senior-level cricket.

Despite having tried to do so without success, one day in July 1822, during an MCC vs Kent match at Lord's, cricket very nearly took a big leap towards its modern form when Willes attempted to apply his roundarm style. Except when he made his delivery, the umpire called a no-ball, at which point Willes apparently had a big ol' hissy fit, stormed off the field, jumped on his horse and rode off, never to play cricket again. (Would the image be as cool if he'd jumped into a mid-range family car and driven off, slowly, because the speed humps in the cricket ground's car park are invariably over-effective, never to play cricket again? Probably not.)

Several cricketing experts have suggested that this story may not be entirely true, because the fashion for ladies' skirts was slimline enough at the time to deliver a reasonable underarm ball. True or not, the story is part of cricket's folklore and it should be politely pointed out that cricketing experts often have an arms-length relationship with the concept of fashion.

Roundarm rises

Willes' hasty exit from his cricket career got people talking. At this point in the development of cricket, batters very much had the upper hand, although the poor state of the pitches by modern standards kept scores relatively low. There were bowlers who could put a wicked spin on an underarm ball, but roundarm bowling was being talked about as a way of evening the balance.

Within a few years, umpires were starting to turn a blind eye to roundarm. By 1828, bowlers could officially have their hands as high as their elbow, which rose to shoulder height seven years later, which basically legalised roundarm bowling.

Bowlers: give them an inch ...

In the eternal battle between good and evil, right and wrong, bowlers and batters, each side is always looking for an advantage over the other. Even though bowlers gained the concession of roundarm, they were not satisfied. Over the next decade, they kept pushing the envelope, raising their arms higher and higher like ecstatic ravers as they released the ball, daring the umpires to declare a no-ball.

In 1845, umpires were given more power and the rules were made even more explicit, but more and more of them were turning a blind eye to bowling arms creeping higher and higher. This was still around a century and a quarter before the television instant replay was introduced, and around a century and three quarters before every spectator had a high-definition video camera in their pockets, so it was very difficult to argue with the umpire's decision if they decided to be relatively relaxed in their interpretation of the rules.

Umpires and anarchy

The distance between the rulebook in the clubhouse and the interpretation at the crease was becoming increasingly problematic. Frankly, it was getting anarchic. By the end of the 1862 season, when Surrey faced off against an England XI, a chap by the name of Edgar Willshire, who had made his debut for Kent in 1850, was given six consecutive no-balls for an overarm action. At this point he, and eight of his teammates, walked off the pitch, forcing play to be abandoned for the rest of the day.

Rather than flounce away on horses, this time around the umpire was replaced so that play could proceed the next day. Willsher, apparently a tall, slim fellow with only one lung, took six for 49.

It's possible that this whole drama was stage-managed to force a change in the rules; if so, the gambit worked. The MCC bowed to the inevitable, and overarm bowling was legalised in time for the 1864 season.

> "Baseball has the great advantage over cricket of being sooner ended."

Irish playwright, critic, polemicist and political activist George Bernard Shaw clearly didn't see the future.

· A LITTLE BOOK OF CRICKET ·

★ JACQUES KALLIS ★ (SOUTH AFRICA)

All-rounder Jacques Kallis made it onto his national Test side for the first time when South Africa hosted England in 1995/96. He scored a single run, didn't bowl and the match was washed out, but that was it, he'd made the team and he stayed there until 2013.

Honourable, solid and often set from the first ball, only two people have scored more Test runs than him and he's one of only four people to have scored centuries in five consecutive Test, One Day and T20 matches. Your bowlers' basic worst nightmare.

Usually lurking attentively at second slip, he's also third on the list of most Test catches. Your batter's basic worst nightmare.

He was also serenely unflappable, seemingly oblivious to sledging and any of the other techniques that fielders love to deploy to put batters off their stride (see page 140). He'd simply step up to the crease, take his position and go about his business, however quickly or slowly the occasion required, no matter what oppositions tried to do to distract him. Your fielder's basic ...

★ FIELDING POSITIONS ★

There are no less than 38 fielding positions in cricket. In a less interesting(/byzantine) sport, these positions would probably be numbered, possibly clockwise starting from the wicketkeeper, and possibly following an outer and an inner clock or something. It might be simpler, but it would be a lot less fun and have a lot less character.

To an extent, similar to changing the length of the pitch into a nice, modern metric measurement, neatening the nomenclature of fielding positions comes down to a big 'Why?' debate. What's in place works; changing it would be disruptive and is unlikely to deliver any benefit to players on the field. They know what they are doing; it's up to the crowd whether they want to learn the finer details of the sport.

It is worth noting that even with the new cricket formats being introduced – seemingly every year, accompanied by fireworks and whizzy graphics – nobody, but nobody, has recommended changing the fielding positions. The positions used change as games and strategies evolve, but the positions themselves stay the same.

There are probably two reasons for this. Firstly, fielding positions are drummed into kids as they learn the fundamentals of the game from about the age of six. It's a shared shorthand that enables the captain to set their field quickly and with as little fuss as possible so that you can get on with the business of sending the batter back to the pavilion with their tail firmly between their legs.

The second reason is that the fielding positions are comprehensive. There's no need to create new positions because they cover all of the ground – and a well-placed field takes into account the format of the game, the type of batter, the weather conditions, the position of game, and what the bowler has in mind. It can basically cover most of the potential outcomes of an over. With 11 fielders trying to cover a field of around 17,000 square metres, it is impossible to have someone in place to cover every possible shot that a batter might play, but a well-placed field can make sure that there's someone nearby to stop the ball running to the boundary or, better yet, snaffle up the catches.

While there are technically 38 named positions that cricketers need to learn, for the casual observer there nine main positions that are worth knowing about: slips, gully, point, cover, third man, fine leg, square leg, mid-wicket and mid-off.

Fielding position 1: Slips

If the batter's right-handed, slip fielders are the folk who stand just to the right of the wicketkeeper (known as 'off-side'), looking to snatch up any errant strokes that the batter makes and stop the ball rolling down to the boundary even when a shot isn't played. Slips require absolute concentration during the bowling process and exceptional reactions after a shot is made.

The word is thought to come from the very earliest days of cricket when fielders would start to stand near the wicket to take advantage of any mistakes, or slips, that the batter made. 'Standing in the slips' sounds better than 'standing in the mistakes'.

Slip fielders are numbered first, second and third, with first slip standing nearest the wicketkeeper. As the fielding team makes its way through the batters, the skill of the batter tends to decline so they are more likely to clip rather than hit the ball. This means that as the fielding team gets into the lower order of batters, more fielders will come in from the outfield and become slips because the batters are less likely to make a big hit and more likely to make a mistake. It's all about probability, though, so the more that a captain knows about the opposition, the more likely they are to set the right number of slips.

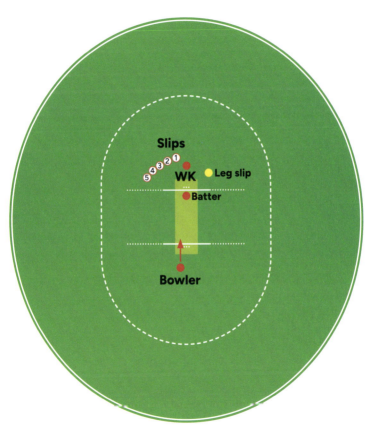

You can usually gauge how confident the fielding team is feeling by how many slips are hovering menacingly around the batter.

Standing on the other side of the wicketkeeper, the leg slip is there to get any balls that the batter steers in that direction. It can be a useful position in which to have a fielder if the batter is under the impression that a sweep shot might be a good idea.

Fielding position 2: Gully

Gully is literally named because it is a narrow channel where the ball can fly in between the slips and the point fielders. Gully fielders stand slightly further round from the slip cordon, almost square to, but slightly behind, the batter. Backward gully stands level with the gully position on the other side but tends to be slightly further away from the wicket.

The reason that there is such a concentration of fielders in this area is basically down to physics: this close to the batter, the ball is likely to be travelling very fast, so there's not a lot of time to react and move very far if you are going to take advantage of a batter's wayward shot. The more fielders you have in this sort of area, the less likely that a mishit ball is going to fly past them and reach the boundary.

The leg gully is the same position on the other side, proving that

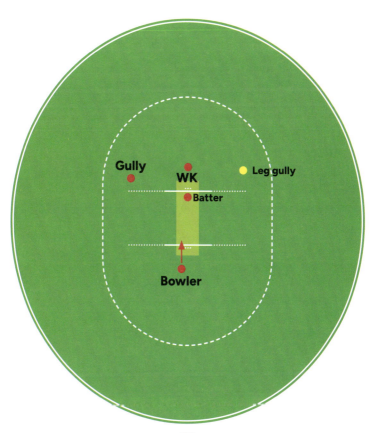

there is a certain logic behind the naming of some of the fielding positions, even if that logic is deeply 18th century. If 'leg' is in the name, you need to be standing on the batter's offside.

Fielding position 3: Point

If anyone ever says that fielding is boring, send them to point. It's the area that sees most of the action, frustrating batters when they decide to step up and try to brush the ball to the side.

Point has three cousins: forward point, which is slightly closer to the bowler; backward point, which is slightly further away; and silly point, which, as the name suggests, is right next to the batter and requires absolutely lightning reflexes. And a helmet. And wicketkeeping pads. And decent insurance.

Point got its name because when you stand there you are facing the point of the bat. It's a pivotal position for the game and the ultimate compliment to your fielding abilities if the captain turns to you and says, "Oi, get your lid on," because they are sending you to where the action's thickest and you are going to need a helmet …

It all looks so serene from the other side of the rope …

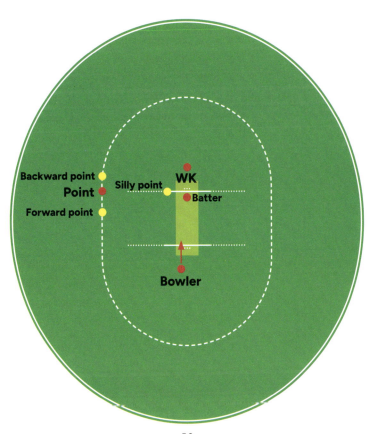

Fielding position 4: Cover

Cover is at about 8 o'clock if you are looking down on a cricket pitch. Fielders are placed there to stop the batter scoring runs with a forward drive, which is probably one of the most natural ways for a batter to hit a ball, and this position also presides over a fair amount of fielding territory. As a result, it's another area that enjoys a lot of fun.

Basically, the slips are there to take a catch if the batter fluffs their shot or doesn't hit the ball quite cleanly; cover is there in case they do.

Cover point, as the name suggests, is a position between cover and point, while extra cover is a little further round towards the bowler. Understanding the batter tends to be what drives the decision to stand at cover, cover point or extra cover. There is also a short extra cover, which is closer to the batter and tends to be used when the fielding team really has their dander up and are expecting to be able to take a catch.

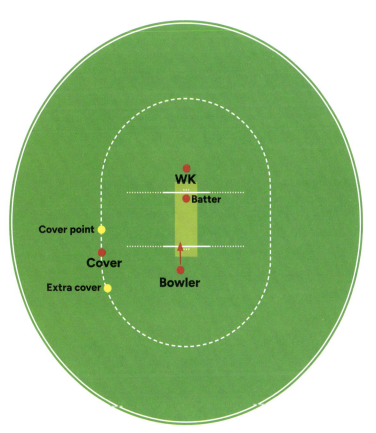

Fielding position 5: Third man

Third man stands out on the boundary to scoop up any balls that go over the slips or the gully and look like they might make their way to the boundary. It's a mostly defensive position, but it covers a lot of ground so you need to be quick on your toes if you are put there.

Third man requires a different set of skills to slip fielding or any of the other positions in the inner circle. Fielders at third man need to be able to track the trajectory of a big hit, time their jumps, take catches, prevent the ball from spilling over the boundary and have a decent throwing arm to get the ball back to the crease and give the team a chance of a run-out.

There's been a lot of focus on fielding technique over the last few years, and much of this work has revolved around what might be called circus skills, combining juggling and gambolling to avoid any part of the body touching the boundary at the same time as the ball. Every run counts.

It might look like fielders at third man are just loitering near the boundary because they've been told off by their captain, but that's just the moments in between.

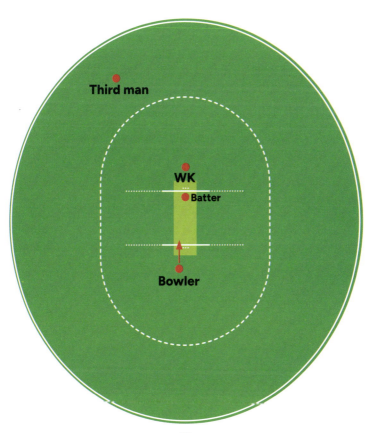

Fielding position 6: Fine leg

Fine leg is the other side of the batter from third man, and it's sometimes where you'll find a bowler trying to get their breath back during their overs off. This, of course, depends on the state of the match. If the batter's trying to have a field day, then there's a decent chance several shots will be put in the direction of fine leg, so fielders in that position need to control their territory to keep the run rate as low as possible.

Technically, if the fielder is out towards the boundary, they are standing at deep fine leg, but when the spinner's doing their thing, fine leg tends to come up to the inner ring and become a short fine leg. Either way, they are there to sweep up the ball and get it back to the wicket as quickly as possible.

There are several positions near to fine leg: long stop is on the boundary directly behind the batting end stumps; long leg is the other side of fine leg, still on the boundary but at about 1 o'clock as you look down on the pitch.

All of these positions exist to stop batters scoring too many runs by being aggressive, so fielders need to be ready to take advantage of any deflections or edges that the batter might make.

Fielding position 7: Square leg

Cricket sounds complex, but actually, when you learn how to decipher it, it's not all that deep (most of the time). Square-leg fielders stand square to the batter on the leg side. It's basically an opportunity to have a natter with the square-leg umpire, keep an eye on the bowler's deliveries to make sure that they are fair (which can be important if there's an opportunity to contest decisions at the very highest level), keep the run rate down and make stupendous catches when the opportunity arises. It's a role, then, that requires a subtle blend of agility, speed, a legal eye and diplomacy.

There is, of course, a deep square leg, which is out towards the boundary, short leg which is right up in the batter's grille, as well as backward and forward square legs which basically correspond to the equivalent on the other side at point.

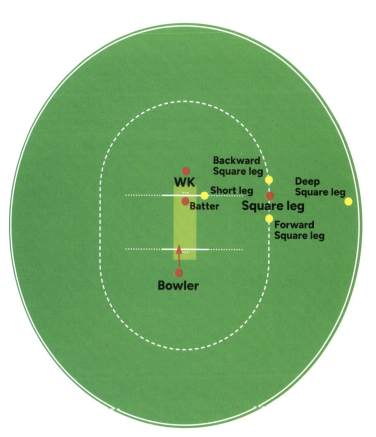

Fielding position 8: Mid-wicket

Mid-wicket is square to the batter on the leg side, just around the edge of the inner circle. It's there to stop the singles and help pressure the batter into making mistakes. It's where a lot of the flying catches happen on that side of the pitch because it's where batters like to put the ball when they are trying to give it some welly.

Closely related to mid-wicket is deep mid-wicket, which is on the same trajectory but out by the boundary, so it comes into play when the fielding team is trying to stop high-order batters putting on a show.

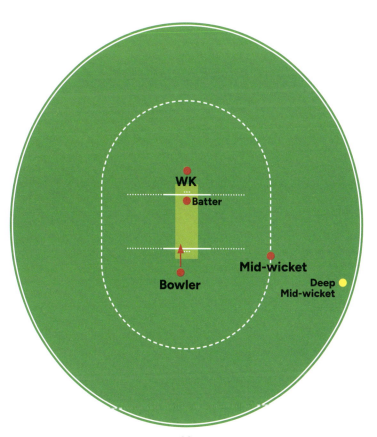

Fielding position 9: Mid-off

Mid-off is where you'll often find the captain skulking during a fielding innings — sufficiently close to the bowler to offer advice and share observations. Again, there's a silly mid-off, which is very close to the batter to take advantage of any errant strokes the batter happens to offer; a deep mid-off, which is towards the boundary; and a long-off, which is right out at the boundary.

Mid-off is basically the spider at the centre of the web that the fielding team is trying to wrap up the batter in. This position is the main point of communication between the fielders and generally has responsibility for ensuring that the field positions are correct and match up to the bowler's plans for the next ball.

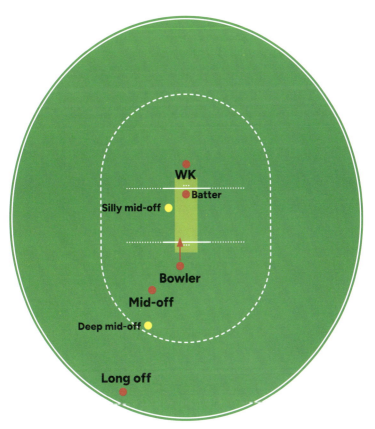

• A LITTLE BOOK OF CRICKET •

★ M.S. DHONI ★
(INDIA)

M.S. Dhoni made his Indian debut in an ODI in 2004, had his test debut in 2005 and three years later became captain of the national Test team, the ODI team and the T20 teams. While they all look like cricket, each format demands different tactics, strategies and stresses. He led India to victory in the 2007 International Cricket Council (ICC) World T20, the 2011 Cricket World Cup and the 2013 ICC Champions Trophy.

It's also worth mentioning that India is one of the most cricket-obsessed countries in the world. The amount of cricket he was playing was exceptional and the level of pressure he was under would have been phenomenal. And still he performed, both as a leader and as a player on the team, making runs and taking catches throughout his tenure.

As former England captain Nasser Hussain observed, when you faced India, it was never over until you got Dhoni out.

★ THE MCC STEPS UP ★ TO THE CREASE

The MCC played at Lord's Old Ground until 1810, when the lease expired, apparently leading to a dispute about rent. Which is weird because Lord's patrons don't appear to have been short of a crust.

Either way, the MCC upped sticks and moved to what is now known as 'Lord's Middle Ground' in St John's Wood. Unfortunately, this land was requisitioned by Parliament in 1813 for the construction of a canal (honestly, what's the actual point in having rich mates?), although fortunately the Middle Ground was said to have been unpopular, so Lord might not have argued too much when he was offered compensation to move somewhere else (which might be the actual point of having rich mates).

So, the MCC upped sticks again and moved to its current home, 200 or so metres to the north-west on the site of a former duck pond. Lord is said to have taken his turf with him and laid it at the new ground.

It's worth noting at this point that while the cricket pitches of the era look nice in oil paintings, in reality, they were what players today would call a bit of a state. Lawnmowers weren't invented until the 1830s and from the sounds of things Lord's didn't invest in their first mowers until the mid-1860s, so prior to this grass maintenance tended to be farmed out to local sheep. Drainage was also rudimentary. This may be part of the reason why the balls were delivered underarm, because faster, overarm throws would be more likely to be wayward on a lumpy pitch. Lord eventually sold his stake in the ground that still holds his name in 1825, retiring in 1830 to a village just down the road from a small hamlet in Hampshire called Hambledon. This might or might not be a coincidence.

The MCC had taken over the governance of cricket from Hambledon in the late 1780s, and it remains closely associated with the global rules of the game, although formal responsibility has moved beyond the remit of the club itself.

★ SPIN BOWLERS ★

Spin bowling is like someone trying to reach nirvana through tantric stretching and then, right at the point of ecstasy, dispatching a ball that has been temporarily excused from the laws of physics. It weaves and meanders through the air in the direction of the batter, leaving psychedelic, paisley traces in its wake, hoping to confuse the opponent into doing something silly. If you squint while watching a spin bowler, you will literally see the outfielders manifest sitars while the slips break into a chorus of 'Lucy in the Sky with Diamonds' as the ball arrives. The fielder at long stop plays the Lowrey Organ. With panache.

This is probably all entirely untrue in our plane of existence, but cricket is played on a lot of different levels, and who knows what's going on with a spin ball – just look at the pretty shapes the ball draws in the air, changing direction in the most unexpected ways.

The weird thing about spin (other than the paisley traces the ball leaves in the air) is that it makes a heavy ball move like a feather. The aerodynamics are deeply strange.

> "Cricket is a beautiful game that connects people and cultures around the world."

West India's Kieron Pollard sums it up nicely.

> "They have come to see me bat, not you bowl,"

W.G. Grace explaining he deserved a do-over after being out first ball.

WAKEY WAKEY, EGG AND BAKEY

The official colours of the MCC are red and yellow, known fondly as 'egg and bacon', which is regularly on display in the club's members' enclosure splashed across exuberant ties and eyebrow-raising blazers. The reason for this is lost to the mists of history, but there is speculation that the colours were chosen as a way of honouring William Nicholson, a member of the MCC who was closely involved in the purchasing of the freehold of the Lord's Ground in 1866. Nicholson made 148 known first-class appearances for the MCC, Middlesex and England, and was also the owner of the Nicholson's Gin Company, which has red and yellow as its corporate colours.

If this is true, it would mean that cricket – which is sometimes thought to be quite a traditionalist sport that is a bit sniffy about anything as crass as being on a sound financial footing – would actually have been one of the earliest sports to embrace corporate sponsorship.

Speaking of footing, if you are invited to the Lord's members paddock, do not, under any circumstances, wear flip-flops.

According to several parts of their website they are – very strictly, and exceptionally Englishly – a No Flip-Flop Zone. You have been warned.

Their policy on Crocs is unclear.

There are several other prohibited items that cannot be worn on match day including ripped or torn vests, offensive garments, camouflage, bare midriffs and singlets. This basically translates to no 1980s rock stars, no 1990s rock stars, no fishermen, Spice Girls or Australians.

No one is sure what they have against Australians.

England have been playing Australia at Lords since 1884, with Australia winning for the first time four years later. In 1934, England won against Australia for the last time until 2009, a 75-year winning streak for the antipodeans.
This is probably just a coincidence.

WOMEN'S CRICKET

Some sports have had a slightly dubious relationship with women who have wanted to play the game, but with the odd comment aside, cricket has basically shrugged and let women get on with it. The first recorded women's match took place back in 1745 involving 'maids' of Bramley and, would you believe it, Hambledon.

Village games continued, particularly across the south of England throughout the 18th and 19th centuries, often attracting fairly good crowds, and by 1890 several women's clubs were set up in the UK and other parts of the world.

By 1926, the Women's Cricket Association was formed in England to bring the game together a bit. It initially had 10 affiliated clubs but this had risen to 123 by 1938, suggesting that there was a healthy appetite for the game even at a point where some other sports were (very) actively discouraging female participation.

It's worth noting that the first Women's Cricket World Cup was held in 1973 (England's women won), and its success paved the way for the men to try something similar in 1975 (England's men did not).

Another interesting note is the discussion around kit. It wasn't until 1997 that female cricketers on the English national team started playing in trousers in the same way as their male counterparts. It's easy to look at that, roll your eyes and mutter something about sexism, but it's worth pointing out that the decision to wear skirts was actually driven by the players rather than any pressure from cricket's male authorities.

In the early 1930s, the England women's team was heading out to Australia and New Zealand for their first tour. They are said to have wanted to come across as both professional and feminine, and settled on a culotte (a cross between a skirt and a wide trouser) to preserve their dignity. Other women's teams around the world followed suit, irrespective of the practicality of skirts when you are trying to field. Skirts were replaced with trousers in 1997.

This is not to say that cricket authorities weren't sexist, instinctively or institutionally (it took 47 years of asking before the women were allowed to play at Lord's for the first time in 1976), or that the people at the top of the game (who were presumably men, by and large) didn't try to influence the decision to wear skirts, but it's interesting that they didn't put anything in the rules to directly make it difficult for women to play how they wanted.

Either way, after seventy years of heading up the women's game, the Women's Cricket Association was disbanded and the England and Wales Cricket Board (ECB) took over in England and Wales in 1998, giving them responsibility for both the male and female versions of the game.

In terms of international operations, the WCA had handed over responsibility to the International Women's Cricket Council in 1958. The IWCC merged with the ICC in 2005, creating a single overall structure for the game.

That 1930s England tour of Australia and New Zealand saw women playing Test cricket for the first time, but the number of Test teams globally has been slowly increasing ever since. Ten women's teams have played test teams. South Africa joined the fray in 1960, followed by India, Pakistan, Ireland, the Netherlands and Sri Lanka. Interestingly, the Netherlands women's team has played Test cricket but the men's have not; of the men's Test teams globally, Afghanistan, Bangladesh and Zimbabwe have not yet competed in a women's Test.

· A LITTLE BOOK OF CRICKET ·

★ SOPHIE ECCLESTONE ★

Sometimes, hopefully mostly in the past, women playing cricket was dismissed with a smile that was supposed to be kind and a pat on the head. In many cases it probably wasn't intentionally patronising, but the effect was the same.

Young Sophie Eccleston played cricket and football with her dad and brother and was starting to develop into a handy bowler, so she did what most people do at school if they have half a talent and asked if she could join the school club. The school's Head presumably gave a smile that was supposed to be kind and handed her the ball … at which point she is said to have bowled out the entire school team and claimed the Head's wicket on the first ball he faced. You'd imagine that the phrase 'emerging talent' started to be used.

Ecclestone star has indeed risen over the last few years. She joined the England Academy squad at 16, made her Women's International T20 and One Day International debuts a year later and her Test debut a year after that. Since then, she's played a lot of cricket in all formats of the game, becoming the joint fastest woman to claim 100 ODI wickets (alongside Australia's Cathryn Fitzpatrick) in 64 matches (although pedants like to point out that Ecclestone actually achieved her feat in 63 innings bowled). She's also currently the second-youngest person to have claimed 10 wickets in a woman's Test.

Player	Years	Catches
Graeme Smith (ICC/SA)	2002–2014	169
Stephen Fleming (NZ)	1994–2008	171
Alastair Cook (ENG)	2006–2018	175
Mark Waugh (AUS)	(1991–2002	181
Steve Smith (AUS)	2010–2024	183
Joe Root (ENG)	2012–2024	193
Ricky Ponting (AUS)	1995–2012	196
Jacques Kallis (ICC/SA)	1995–2013	200
Mahela Jayawardene (SL)	1997–2014	205
Rahul Dravid (ICC/IND)	1996–2012	210

★ WORLD TEST CATCHERS ★

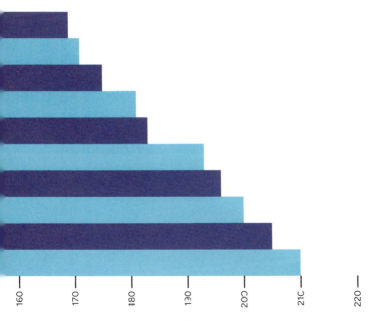

★ WICKETS – SO GOOD ★
THEY ADDED A THIRD

The aim of cricket is to either protect or attack the wicket, depending on which side of the game you are on at a given moment. What this means is that the wicket is central to the game of cricket.

The word 'wicket' itself is probably derived from a simple type of gate known, astonishingly, as a wicket gate – basically a bunch of vertical slats held together by a cross piece or two with hinges down one side. So, essentially, what we've all be calling a gate for all these years is technically a wicket gate. You were probably today-years-old when you found this out; you're very welcome, as they say on social media. Sweet Lord, I wish they'd stop.

The true story of how a type of gate came to be used in the game of cricket is sadly lost to history, but the likelihood is something simple, like the fact that it makes a satisfying noise when hit by a leather and horsehair ball – and proto-cricketers took it from there.

Originally, a cricket wicket only had two stumps, but this was changed in 1775. The stupendously monikered Surrey bowler Lumpy Stevens is said to have bowled three consecutive balls through the gap between the two stumps. If you've ever spent any time with a bowler, you can imagine how grumpy this made Lumpy, so they invented the middle stumpy. Sorry (not sorry). It's worth noting that Lumpy Stevens was bowling to a Hambledon batter by the name of John Small at the time he achieved this feat. If they had been playing together, there's a risk that the commentators could have ended up announcing that it was Small and Lumpy in the crease, which would probably have led to a lot of very juvenile giggling.

Moving swiftly on, with the third stump added to the wicket in 1775, the wicket has remained the same for 250 years now, which is fairly amazing when you stop and think about it. Sure, at the top end of the sport these days they have LED lights to make it really clear when the bails have come off, but a quarter of a millennium without significant change is very impressive.

WHAT THE FORMAT?

Another way that Cricket can seem quite complicated is regarding the actual formats of the game. With football, rugby and golf, no matter what the ins and out are of the various competitions, the game itself is generally the same – 90 minutes, 80 minutes or indeterminable. Cricket, on the other hand, seems to have a bewildering array of formats. There are ODIs, T20s, One Dayers, Tests, Twenty20s, 20Twentys, 20/20s, The One Hundred, One Day Internationals and First Class Tests to name but a few.

The reality is, though, that there are only four main formats you need to get your head around. They come with a lot of different names, but basically you only need to think about: The Hundred, 20Twenty, One Day and Test.

The Hundred

The Hundred is the new kid on the block and is only played in England and Wales at this point. It is called The Hundred because each side gets 100 balls to try and score as many runs as possible. It's brash and deeply unsubtle and only takes a couple of hours to play, making it perfect for a summer evening where you amble to the cricket ground after work and watch some people try and get the ball over the pavilion as many times as they can.

The Hundred has done away with overs, replacing them with sets of five balls. Why? Because the people that created it are very keen to show that they are a brash upstart that doesn't play by the old rules. Also, 6 doesn't go into 100.

20Twenty

If there's a wee bit too much caffeine and sugar in The Hundred, the 20Twenty format gallops along at a decent lick and encourages batters to play their strokes and chase the big runs. It's called 20Twenty because each team gets 20 overs, which translates to around 400 balls, assuming that the bowlers are having a decent day and not bowling too many wides.

20Twenty emerged at the start of the 2000s and has led to the creation of several popular global leagues such as Australia's Big Bash and the Indian Premier League (IPL) which have really increased visibility and interest in cricket over the last two decades.

Basically, if The Hundred is a two-minute punk song, 20Twenty is a slightly more traditional three-and-a-half minute pop tune.

One Day Matches

The clue's in the name on this one; One Day Matches give each team 50 overs and are designed to take around one day to play. The benefit of a one-day match is that it gives teams the chance to really test all the different parts of the game, which can ebb and flow over the course of a long summer afternoon.

County Championships and One Day Internationals (ODIs) follow this format and it's basically the mainstay of the cricketing calendar. It's cricket equivalent of what you hear on a 'best of' classical music radio station; considered, without being too challenging.

Test Cricket

Finally, there are the Tests, which can last anything up to five days and really, really test a team's mettle. Because of this length, being specific about the number of overs doesn't really work — it's basically a question of playing cricket until the cricket is played.

Each team has two innings, so they have two opportunities to showcase both their batting and their fielding prowess and it's generally a test of patience, stamina and intelligence: If your batters go out all guns blazing, they might put together a big score, but a collapse is equally possible. It's a subtle game, where winning involves a range of different skills from each team's captain – knowing how the ball is deteriorating; how the pitch might change with different weather conditions; whether your third batter is feeling confidence or the pressure …

It's cricket in its full orchestral glory, full of quiet bits and noisy bits that build up over three, four or five days … until being called off by rain.

Because the risk of rain stopping play just as a game is reaching the peak of its crescendo is an unfortunate reality of the summertime on a small island that is nestled between the North Sea and the Atlantic Ocean. But what is love without risk …?

 THE COVERS

Cricket is a joyful sport, immediately making you think of long summer days watching the run rate slowly tick over while long, cold drinks evaporate in the heat moderately more quickly. There is one piece of equipment that is central to the game in Britain that no one really likes to talk about, because no one really wants to acknowledge its necessity: the covers.

Covers appear to have been introduced into the game in 1788. We know this because while the 1788 revision of the *Laws of Cricket* has been lost to history, the 1796 version exists and it indicates that covers became a thing eight years earlier. This rule simply stated that the pitch could be covered if both captains agreed.

This rule stayed in place for around a century, at which point it was made illegal to cover the wicket during a match or for 24 hours before a county match.

From the modern perspective, covering the wicket when it looks like it might rain is simply common sense. Pitches can become treacherous when they are wet, and the ball's behaviour can move beyond entertainingly erratic and into downright dangerous, so making it illegal to cover the pitch seems like the opposite of health and safety gone mad.

But one rule in cricket has changed since the game was formalised: overarm bowling (see page 45). If you are sidling up to the wicket and bowling an underarm ball at a batsman, then a bit of mud isn't too much of a concern. If you are running in at full pelt trying to send the bales to Wales (better yet, the batter to their constituent matter), then a slippery run-up is not really helping you do your job or provide a spectacle.

There is now some seriously impressive technology that goes into cricket covers, and they are deployed by ground teams that are drilled to respond more quickly than a Formula One pit crew. Most cricket fans know that if the weather is even remotely dodgy, it's worth keeping quarter of an eye on the covers so that they are ready to get to the bar if it looks like the covers are going on.

★ BALLS ★

Cricket balls are not made out of rock, although it can feel like it if you've ever muffed up a catch or ambled out of the pavilion during a match without taking due care and attention.

Cricket is not a winter sport; it's played during the summer when the ground is mostly hard. As a result, the ball isn't designed to be particularly bouncy or do anything especially clever beyond the complex vagaries of basic aerodynamics. This means that the design that was developed in the 1770s is pretty much what is still used today.

When Charles Goodyear developed his method of vulcanising rubber in the mid-19th century and revolutionised football and rugby balls, the cricket ball remained the same. Material science has not been needed to make the ball lighter or more waterproof, nor have enhanced design technologies been needed to change it aerodynamically so that it bounces more consistently.

The first cricket ball did what it needed to do, and, with the exception of a couple of extra colours and a microchip here and there, it still does exactly what it needs to do: move at terrifying speed, twist and turn at the best bowlers' whims, and deteriorate at a more or less consistent rate as a match progresses.

Duke and Son, master craftsmen of Kent, received a royal patent to produce cricket balls in 1775. In 1780, they introduced the six-seamed ball, which gave bowlers more grip and made the performance more consistent – and that's been pretty much it. Duke and Son have been through various guises, and they no longer produce balls in Kent, but nearly a quarter of a millennium later, they are still producing cricket balls.

Kookaburra Sport came along in 1890 and then Sanspareils Greenlands (SG) joined the party in 1931. There are subtle differences in the way that each ball behaves in different environments, but, by and large, these are only apparent to people who either deliver them or try to face them down.

With 250 years of history, construction is fairly simple: All professional cricket balls have a cork core which is then wrapped with several layers of yarn. This is then given an outer casing of lacquer-coated leather, which is red for Test matches, white for T20s (introduced in 1977 with Kerry Packer's short-lived World Series Cricket revolution) and pink for day-night matches (arriving in 2015). Test and T20 balls have white stitching holding the outer casing together, while pink balls have green stitching for contrast against floodlights.

In the men's game, the cricket ball weighs between 155.9 g and 163 g and has a circumference of between 22.4 cm and 22.9 cm. In the women's game, the balls weigh between 140 g and 151 g with a circumference of between 21 cm and 22.5 cm. Cricket balls for junior cricketers weigh between 133 g and 144 g and have a circumference of between 20.5 cm and 22.0 cm.

While cricket may look like a relaxing sport and watching cricket a relaxing pastime, you need to keep your wits about you because whatever the size or colour, you don't want to be hit by a cricket ball.

• A LITTLE BOOK OF CRICKET •

"You don't get good players out by sledging."

Pakistan's Imran Khan is absolutely right. Mostly.

· A LITTLE BOOK OF CRICKET ·

★ SHANE WARNE ★
(AUSTRALIA)

The word 'larrikin' is often bandied about when Shane Warne is discussed – and generally with good reason. It's a word that's come to describe someone who is rowdy, doesn't stand on ceremony but is basically good natured at heart. There are two other words that should be used when thinking about Warne's career: the first is 'entertainer'; the other is 'phenomenon'.

Warne announced his presence on the international cricket scene with what has come to be known as the 'Ball of the Century', or more simply 'That Ball'. Warne had played in 11 Test matches up to that point but hadn't really set the world on fire, but his first ball on day two of an Ashes Test at Old Trafford was what made people sit up and notice. Delivered after a short run-up to experienced England batter Mike Gatting, the ball headed down past the off stump before changing its mind and neatly taking out Gatting's leg stump.

You can talk about spin and the Magnus effect and physics as much as you like, but he should not have been able to make that ball do that. Gatting stood at his crease in disbelief, staring after the ball. If he hadn't been encouraged off the pitch, he'd probably still be standing and staring after the ball 30 years on.

This was the first of 34 dismissals during the course of the 1993 Ashes series and set the tone for Warne's international career:

moments of absolute brilliance punctuating a base level that was merely exceptionally good. He played in 145 tests for Australia, taking 708 wickets and contributing more than 3,000 runs – each of which was scored at the most irritating point in the match from the opposition's point of view.

Shane Warne: A pint, a grin, and an ability to turn a game on its head.

Shane Warne holds the world record for scoring the most runs without making a century – 3,154 runs.

THE ASHES OF HISTORY

The Ashes is a series of five Test matches, held every two years between Australia and England. To be more accurate, the Ashes is generally a series of five Test matches, held mostly every two years that tends to give the Australians the opportunity to teach the English how to play cricket. Or at least that's how it feels.

The reality is a little more evenly balanced. Well, at least a little more nuanced. The Ashes have been contested 73 times since the 1882/83 series, with Australia winning 34 times, England winning 32 times, and honours even seven times. This translates to Australia winning 47% of the time and England winning 44% of the time, which is basically okay.

The reason that it feels more like our Antipodean chums win far more often than this is that in actual fact they do. In terms of the 361 individual Tests that have made up the 73 series, Australia have won 152 times while England have won 111 times. Essentially, it's 42% to Australia, 31% to England. Draws are the order of the day 27% of the time.

So, basically, it's nuanced – either in Australia's favour or very much in Australia's favour.

· A LITTLE BOOK OF CRICKET ·

★ DENIS COMPTON ★
(ENGLAND)

Denis Compton got his first cap against New Zealand in 1937 at the tender age of a little over 19, and is still England's third youngest Test debutant. He quickly became a mainstay of the England team, scoring his first century just under a year later, and is still the youngest England player to score a Test century.

Basically, he was a handy chap to have on the team for the next two decades, although he lost some of the best of those years to World War II. He played with an insouciance that might be familiar today: he was at the crease to play cricket, have fun and entertain. The only mark against his cricketing prowess is his alleged tendency to run people out, with those around him in the dressing room suggesting that a call for a run from Compton was simply the start of a negotiation.

His talent in some ways was a catalyst for social changes. Noted to be somewhat absent-minded off the pitch, Compton hired Bagenal Harvey to manage his correspondence and Harvey quickly evolved into the first sports agent, representing several of the leading cricketers, footballers and athletes of the day. Harvey set up Compton's lucrative endorsement of Brylcreem, an ad campaign that was so successful that a generation of British men never had a hair out of place.

Many cricketers while away the winter months trudging to and from winter net sessions in drafty school halls, snatching furtive glances at quagmires that used to be cricket pitches and willing spring to come around. Not Compton. He had a side hustle as a winger for Arsenal, and was involved with teams that won the league championship title (the old First Division) in 1937/8, the First Division in 1948 and the FA Cup in 1950. In total, he made 54 league appearances for the Gunners, finding the net 15 times including on debut. A chap needs a hobby after all.

Tales of Compton are legion. It is said that he turned up at Old Trafford for a Test against South Africa in 1955 without his kit. We've all done it. Most of us would swear, blag teammates for our kits and then hope there's a local shop that stocks clean boxes in the right size.

Compton wasn't most people though. Realising his mistake, he stomped down to Old Trafford's Museum of Cricket, borrowed an old bat and then went out to play. England lost by three wickets, but he was the highest scoring player for either team with innings of 158 and 71.

A few years later, English cricket's great and good gathered to celebrate Compton's 70th birthday. As they sat down to a presumably sumptuous meal, the guest of honour received a phone call from his mum informing him that it was his 69th rather than his 70th birthday. Absent minded, but awfully good at cricket.

HOW THE ASHES CAME TO BE

The Ashes is one of those gloriously wonky cricketing stories. Basically, Australia and England had been playing each other since 1877, but on their ninth Test in 1882, Australia snatched a famous victory from the English at the Oval. It was the first time that England had lost on home soil. It was only by seven runs, but still. The very idea. It is said that the match was so exciting that during the closing stages, someone in the crowd died of a heart attack and another bit clean through the handle of his umbrella. Which is possibly the most English reaction to stress that the world has ever seen.

Over the next few days, the Victorian society was abuzz with talk of the match, and two newspapers went so far as to write mock obituaries that declared the death of English cricket. Interestingly at the time there was a national debate going on about cremation, which was still illegal. The author of one of the obituaries was giving publicity to the campaign to have cremation legalised (which was eventually achieved in 1902), so their tongue-in-cheek declaration about the cremation of the body of English cricket was serving a double purpose: lamenting the sad demise of English pride and keeping cremation on the news agenda.

But words carry, and when the England team set off to Australia a few months later for the 1882/83 tour, captain Ivo Bligh declared in the press that his intention was to set forth to "regain those ashes", with Australian captain Billy Murdoch stating that he would defend those ashes on behalf of Australia. The press lapped it up, the 'A' became capitalised, and a simple cricket tour was transubstantiated into nothing less than a mythical quest for the Ashes.

England took two of the three Tests in the series and, at the end of it all, Bligh was presented with a small urn that is said to possibly contain the ashes of a cremated bail.

It's never a straight line

Except there's a certain amount of doubt about whether the urn on display at the MCC since 1927 is actually the container that Bligh was presented with in 1883. There is apparently good evidence that the original urn was simply an emptied silver perfume bottle presented to Bligh as a joke at the end of a friendly match in Australia that took place before the actual Test had even begun. There are also stories about the contents of the urn: it might be a cremated stump, it could potentially be the outer casing of a cricket ball, or even, oddly, the ashes of Bligh's future mother-in-law's veil (it's convoluted and we've probably got better things to talk about).

But, in a lot of ways, who cares? It's a great story. We know that the urn on display was presented to the MCC for safekeeping by Bligh's widow in 1927, which gives it pretty good provenance, and whether it's 100 years old or 140 years old, it has come to represent the cricketing rivalry between the two nations that keeps people on the edge of their seats to this day.

· A LITTLE BOOK OF CRICKET ·

★ SIR ALASTAIR COOK ★
(ENGLAND)

We can start with the world-record 159 successive Test caps, and we could probably stop there as well, but there is plenty more to Alastair Cook's career. He marked himself out as a batter with potential in 2005 at the age of 20 by scoring 214 for Essex against Australia. He was the youngest English player to reach 7,000 Test runs and made more Test centuries than any other English player. In the 2010/11 Ashes, he scored 766 runs in seven innings, which is the sort of stat that would make an Australian doff the baggy green. The 263 he ground out of Pakistan in 2015 is the third-longest innings ever played and is probably still giving bowlers nightmares.

His temperament made him perfectly suited to Test cricket: able to ride out the good balls and punish the bad ones. He scored a century in his final Test innings, and it's hard to see a more perfect way to bow out (although he enjoyed another five years in first-class cricket with Essex).

★ CRICKET AND THE WEATHER ★

When it comes to the English weather, with the best will in the world, cricket is tricksy. In most people's heads, cricket has convinced you that it's always sunny when the game is played: it's an eternal, indolent May day with clear blue skies for miles. T-shirts and shorts. Tasteful linen suits with, possibly questionable, cravats. Fresh cucumber sandwiches served on fold-out picnic tables embellished with neat, ironed, gingham tablecloths. Pimms and lemonade. Cucumber sandwiches.

And it's not really true. Cricket seasons run from late spring to early autumn, and it can be awfully cold in either of the months that bookend the season. Cold and grey and windy, and – sometimes – even snowy in May; dank and dark in September.

The trick that cricket plays is that the game stops for rain. This means that if you watch it on the television, it's never raining. Sure, sometimes the commentators get caught in a shower, but anything more significant and the coverage switches to somewhere else, where it's sunny and all's right with the world. Or it moves over to repeats of classic games from a decade ago. The picture quality might not be as good, but nine times out of 10 it was sunny.

With every other sport, when the seasons change, you'll get an email or two from a sports shop asking if your gear is ready for the change in season. Have you got your waterproofs? Are the lugs or studs on your boots long enough? Is it time to layer up?

Not cricket. Everyone knows that it's always played when it's sunny. Because that's what you see on the telly.

As a result of this, you can guarantee that when the first game of the season trundles around there will be a couple of spectators who leap out of the car in sandals and sunglasses, full of the joys of spring, before quickly realising their colossal mistake and beating a hasty retreat to the nearest purveyor of rugs, fleeces and handwarmers. You can find them in the clubhouse throughout April, usually huddled around a mug of tea next to a radiator. If you listen closely, you'll hear them mutter through blue lips, "It's cricket … it's not supposed to be cold … but it was cold … so very cold …"

And that's just the spectators. What about the kids playing it? If they've got any foresight, they might have found a white base layer in the bottom of the cupboard, but if the parents are getting caught out, what chance have the kids got?

Then, of course, there's the small matter of the ball. A cricket ball is a solid bit of kit on the best of days, but if the mercury is struggling to get into double figures, then trying to catch even an old cricket ball is basically like trying to catch an orb of iron. That's been set in concrete.

Cricket is tricksy. If you are watching, wear layers and keep gloves nearby until at least mid-May. If you are playing, always have a base layer handy. And possibly a secret pair of long johns. Thermal long johns.

> Daryll Cullinan was responsible for one of the more bizarre hold ups in play when, playing in a Castle Cup match, he flambéed Roger Telemachus for a six-over deep mid-wicket and the ball sailed into a spectator's barbecue to find itself lodged between the coals and some gently grilling calamari. When the ball was discovered, it took 10 minutes to cool down sufficiently for the umpires to attempt to remove the grease and seafood from its slow-cooked leather. Remarkably, after the de-greasing, play was resumed with the same ball.

"Serious cricket is war minus the shooting,"

suggested George Orwell. He made similar comments about virtually every sport, although history does not record his opinions about mixed martial arts.

· A LITTLE BOOK OF CRICKET ·

★ IMRAN KHAN ★
(PAKISTAN)

Becoming the captain of Pakistan changed Imran Khan from someone who could hit the ball into a leader who dismantled oppositions throughout the 1980s. He was as famous for his off-pitch exploits as for what he achieved with a ball in hand – but that shouldn't take away from how good a cricketer he made himself.

We can look at the stats and the records if you like, but possibly one of the best examples of Khan's character came during a 1989 ODI between Pakistan and India. Kris Srikkanth had stabilised India's innings, taking the score from 18–2 to 66–3, but was given out leg before wicket (LBW) from a ball from Waqar Younis. This was in the days before it was possible to go upstairs, so once the umpire had raised the finger, Srikkanth had to go. In a moment of imperious sportsmanship, Khan overruled the umpire, calling Srikkanth back to the crease, because, despite initially appealing, the Pakistani captain didn't think the decision was a good one.

It was a thoroughly decent thing to have done, and it might have led to Khan being absolutely pilloried in the newspapers the next day were it not for the fact that Srikkanth was caught behind on the very next ball. The universe balances the scales. Sometimes.

★ WHAT EVEN IS COW CORNER? ★

There is one part of the cricket pitch that tends to attract bewildered looks from the uninitiated: cow corner. Cow corner is the region of the pitch at about 5 o'clock from where a right-handed batter is playing. It is thought to originate from the playing fields of Dulwich College, where a herd of cattle once chewed the cud near the cricket pitch (it's now a wine merchant, which might be deemed progress). Historically, batters have sent the ball to cow corner when they take a big, often uncontrolled, slog. This is also where the term 'agricultural shot' comes from – something that you hear being uttered, somewhat sniffily, in the commentary box (when they are not sniggering about Small and Lumpy in the crease).

Strangely, with the rise of shorter formats of the game that encourage big hits and bigger risks, aiming for cow corner is less frowned on than it used to be. It's risky, but go big or go home. It can be a good place to aim if you want to keep the scoreboard mooving.

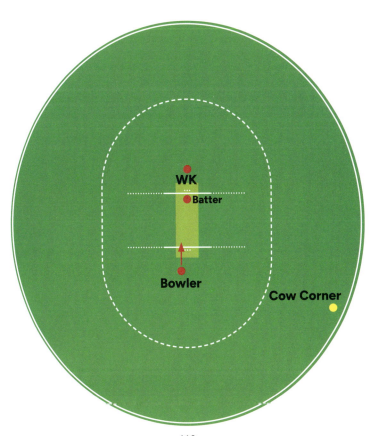

· A LITTLE BOOK OF CRICKET ·

★ BEN STOKES ★
(ENGLAND)

Ben Stokes is very much a cricketer who reflects the age. An exceptionally useful player in a variety of positions, he has developed into an excellent captain of the England Test side, making bold decisions and willing to shoulder more than his share of the blame if those decisions don't work out. As a player, a leader and a sportsperson, he always seems to remember that cricket is a form of entertainment and, on the pitch, seems to focus on the philosophy that it's better to burn out than fade away.

He has wholeheartedly embraced the Bazball ethos during his time as England captain, chasing every ball with puppy-like enthusiasm. Sometimes it works out, sometimes it doesn't. Sometimes, those outside the dressing room suggest that a more strategic approach might be more likely to deliver victory. They might occasionally be right, but would it be as much fun?

What's he's created is an England team that has the freedom to play the game without constraint. That might raise the eyebrows of purists, but people are queuing out the door to see his teams play, which is good news for the sport's future.

★ WHY ARE THERE ★ SIX BALLS TO AN OVER?

In an ideal world, there would be a definitive answer to the question of why there are six balls in an over. Unfortunately, the real world is complicated and messy and full of things that we all just have to learn to accept. Frankly, there are six balls in an over just because. While six seems like a deeply inefficient number when we are all used to working in decimals, six is actually, simply, the perfect number.

There are several different types of specialist bowlers, but one thing that's consistent is that on a hot summer's day, running up and contorting your body into a bowling position is actually fairly tiring (even if you are only a mooching spinner who does all the hard work on a different plane of reality). An average fast bowler can run up to 20 km during a day's play, which is only fractionally shorter than a half marathon, so putting it into short bursts of six balls is probably only fair if they are going to keep up their performance.

Cricket is all about the numerous little contests that go on during play – and one of the key contests is between a specific bowler and a particular batter. It really is all in the detail, and these contests tend to need six balls to play out.

It can be as simple as bowler throws leather ball at stumps while batter tries to swat it with a solid lump of willow. Often, though, there's a whole lot more going on. For a start, if they are facing a fast bowler rampaging in to bowl the ball at around 90 miles per hour, it is estimated the batter has around 0.3 seconds to react to the ball as it leaves the bowler's hand. They then have a further 0.3 seconds for the message to get from their brain to the various parts of their body that they need to strike the ball and 0.6 of a second to select a shot and react. With so little time to react, a lot of the work is already done before the bowler's even started their run-up.

Take an average over …

Ball 1

The batter takes their position, the bowler looks at that position and thinks to themselves, *That batter is standing just a smidge to the left, exposing their off stump. I can bowl straight at it now and have a small chance of taking the wicket. But the batter's good, so if I bowl a couple of balls just a touch down the leg side, I might be able to nudge them to go a little further that way, get that stump a little more open. I'll get them on ball three once they've exposed the target a little more.*

Meanwhile the batter is thinking, *I'm going to stand just a tiny bit to the left and see if I can lure him into thinking that I'm exposing my off stump. That way, they'll waste a couple of balls trying to nudge me a little further that way.*

The batter connects nicely with the ball, which races away across a dry outfield. The two batters scamper between the wickets and back again for a comfortable two runs.

Ball 2

The bowler thinks to themselves, *I now need to pull the angry face to pretend that I'm annoyed about those two runs, but secretly I'm overjoyed that the batter has indeed shifted their position a smidge to the left, because it proves that he's falling for my plan. One more ball, one more nudge, one more sliver of gap between them and their off stump, and I'll send them back to the pavilion. They'll rue the day that they had the audacity to face me. Bwah ha ha, ha ha.* Because all fast bowlers are megalomaniacs.

Meanwhile, at the other end of the pitch, the batter is thinking, *I like this one; their angry face is terrible. I'm going to leave the next ball to see if I'm right and they are trying to entice me to come further down the leg side, the naughty minx ... Wait, what did they just say to their captain? I couldn't hear it over the chuntering from the wicketkeeper ... Probably nothing ...*

To the delight of the crowd, the batter makes a mighty leap forward and ostentatiously misses the ball, which sails past the bat and safely into a fielder's hands. No run.

Ball 3

That swing-and-a-miss was a little too theatrical for my liking, thinks the bowler. I think the batter's on to my cunning plan. We are nearly halfway through the over. Do I carry on or do I change approach? I know, I'll chuck something harmless at them, let them have their four and then deal with them on the next ball.

Underneath their helmet, the batter grimaces to themselves, checks the field position and tries to work out what comes next. Out of the corner of their eye, they see the captain smirk at the bowler, the wicketkeeper makes a pointed remark and all the fielders take a miniscule step forward. The batter is focused on the game and what the bowler's up to, but they also can't help but picture the fielders with knives and forks in their hands as the bowler steams towards the wicket.

It's an inviting ball, but the batter doesn't step up to it. A second dot ball.

Ball 4

The bowler is thinking that the batter is leaving too much of the off stump visible, but they've done it in a really obvious way. *They are going to try a reverse sweep on me and I am now irritated because what I thought was an opportunity actually turns out to be little more than cheap theatrics from my chum with the bat. I wonder if they realise about the rough patch?*

The batter tries to keep their head, thinking, *The bowler is very sweet trying to entice me to leave my off stump exposed, but I might have tipped my hand just then ... The skipper just had another word with them ... I think they've worked out that I know that they know, but I need to decide quickly whether they know that I know that they know that I know or whether it's just that I know that they know ... But what if I'm wrong? What if they don't know at all? I've only faced them once before. What if I'm misreading their reactions. What if ...?*

The rough patch does its job, the ball skids ever so slightly, forcing the batter to hastily correct their position and play a defensive stroke that was fielded neatly. A third ball with no runs.

Ball 5

The bowler thinks to themselves, *I looked in the batter's eye when I came down the pitch, and I saw confusion. I think they think that they know that I know that they know that I know, but they don't know if I know. The seed of doubt that we planted in their head in the second ball has grown — grown into a mighty oak of turmoil: they don't know what to do, and better yet, they don't know what I'm going to do. So I'm going to try a yorker.*

The batsman, a single bead of sweat trickling down their brow, watches the bowler as they walk slowly to their mark under the beating June sun. They try to judge the bowler's thoughts by the set of their shoulders while ignoring the friendly comments coming from the wicketkeeper.

The bowler turns and begins their run, the batter's eyes widen ... the expected ball didn't materialise; instead, the batter is undone by a well-disguised yorker that slips under their bat and skittles the stumps. The bowler has a victim.

> ### Ball 6
>
> *And that is how you take down a middle-order batter,* thinks the bowler, celebrating with the rest of the team. One last ball in the over. *The skipper says it's spin next, so I'll just soften the newbie with something unplayable that jumps up around their armpit ...*
>
> The new batter takes their position, knowing that they just have to survive the next ball before their battle really commences.

The point is that when it comes to overs, five balls is too few to develop the kind of battle between batter and bowler that cricket thrives on. It would also mean that much more time would be wasted with resetting the field between each over to take into account different bowling styles and strategies.

Fast bowling is also incredibly physical. Making an over last for seven balls would be very taxing, even for professional sportspeople, particularly when a Test can last up to five days and bowlers have to weave their magic over two innings.

So, it seems that the best answer to the question of why there are six balls in an over is simply, in the majority of cases, that six balls is the right number.

· A LITTLE BOOK OF CRICKET ·

★ FRED TRUEMAN ★
(ENGLAND)

One of the wonderful things about cricket is that there's always a chance that you could get roped into a game. Fred Trueman started bowling at the age of four and turned out for his local team for the first time when he was eight (it may have helped that his father was captain of the team). He played village cricket throughout his childhood.

By 14, his talent was starting to become clear and he eventually caught the eye of the Yorkshire county set-up. Opportunities were slow to come, though, with Yorkshire not really interested in having an out-and-out fast bowler, which is what Trueman undoubtedly was.

He was lucky, though, that the England team was in the doldrums in the early 1950s, having been decimated by Australian fast bowlers in their last three series. England needed a fast bowler, and Trueman came rushing up.

In his debut Test, against India in 1952, he took three of the first four wickets, helping reduce India to none for four (yes, that's England reducing India to none for four). Later in the same series he took a blistering eight for 21 as India were bowled out for 58.

It wasn't all plain sailing though. Trueman's instinctive Yorkshire bluntness, sharpened by an acerbic wit, often put him on the wrong side of the authorities at national and county level which meant that despite his obvious talent he was often overlooked. On the upside, this challenged him to become a more complete bowler, and meant that where opportunities started to arise he had a range of balls that made him into a legend.

He went on to become the first player to take 300 Test wickets back in the days when Tests weren't as common, and is still the tenth-fastest bowler to reach the 300-wicket mark, achieving it in 65 matches.

Every few years a player comes along and comes to define English cricket for their decade or so at the crease. Right now it's Ben Stokes, before that it was Andrew Flintoff, then Ian Botham and then Trueman. It could have been very different though: when he was 12 he was hit in the groin with a cricket ball while not wearing a box. As a result, he ended up being off school for the best part of a year and nearly lost his leg. There might be a subtle lesson in that.

Never short of an opinion, but always funny and warm hearted, Trueman enjoyed a 13-year Test career and played top flight cricket with Yorkshire for 19 years. (After he retired, he also popped up briefly for six limited-over matches for exotic Derbyshire.)

Trueman's daughter was briefly married to the son of Hollywood actress Raquel Welch. Which probably just goes to show.

★ FAST BOWLERS ★

Fast bowling is a peculiar mix of extreme subtlety and raw aggression. Like a thrash metal song from the mid-1990s, it's basically trying to bludgeon the batter into submission before suddenly and unexpectedly breaking into a melody. Before going back to bludgeoning the batter into submission.

Despite the long run-ups, you never quite know when the bowler is going to dispatch the ball, so batters pretty much have to do their research, play the averages, and keep their wits about them. Because one of the most devastating things that a fast bowler can do is bowl what is technically called 'a slightly slower one'.

As a fast bowler, you are reading the batter as much as the condition of the pitch and the state of the ball. You are looking for the moment when the batter's body language tells you that they think they've worked you out – because that's when you change, when you add that little bit of extra spin that makes the ball twist through the gap between the bottom of the bat and the ground and smash into the stumps.

SIGHTSCREENS

One of the weird things that you spot at most cricket grounds is the sightscreen. A great big white fence on wheels that from most perspectives doesn't really do much except sometimes teeter nerve-rackingly when the breeze is high. They may look weird, but they're important.

The sightscreen is placed behind the bowler, and it removes distractions for the batter, which is important when they are facing a ball that can be delivered at the best part of 90 miles per hour. They are plain white so that batters can focus on what the bowler is doing during their run up and to help them track the ball as it makes its way through the air. There are two so that teams can change ends between overs.

Baseball has something similar with the batter's eye screen – a contrasting colour that lets the batter see what the pitcher's up to.

There are a lot of rules and etiquette in cricket, but the main one that outsiders need to follow is that you don't move anywhere near the batter's sightscreen when a bowler's steaming in.

> "Cricket is a game that requires skill, strategy, and a bit of luck. It keeps you on your toes and tests your character."

England's Joe Root is right about everything except the amount of luck. You make your own, but you always need more than a bit.

Player	Years	100s
Alastair Cook (ENG)	2006–2018	33
Mahela Jayawardene (SL)	1997–2014	34
Brian Lara (ICC/WI)	1990–2006	34
Sunil Gavaskar (IND)	1971–1987	34
Younis Khan (PAK)	2000–2017	34
Rahul Dravid (ICC/IND)	1996–2012	36
Kumar Sangakkara (SL)	2000–2015	38
Ricky Ponting (AUS)	1995–2012	41
Jacques Kallis (ICC/SA)	1995–2013	45
Sachin Tendulkar (IND)	1989–2013	51

• A LITTLE BOOK OF CRICKET •

★ WORLD TEST CENTURIES ★

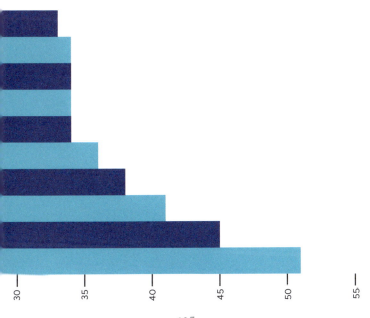

· A LITTLE BOOK OF CRICKET ·

★ ANDREW FLINTOFF ★
(ENGLAND)

There were legendary sledgers and banterers in the past, but Freddie Flintoff arrived on the scene just as camera and microphones were becoming good enough to give us an insight into what was happening on the pitch during the match. It was like a nature documentary, offering a glimpse of a world that had previously been hidden to anyone but the players. You half-expected to hear a voiceover proclaim in hushed tones, "… And here we see, standing at third slip, a young Andrew Flintoff, named 'Freddie' by his school friends because of his alleged resemblance to Fred Flintstone. He's drawing in a breath, so he's about to chirp, to make what might be called a quip, that will really wind up the batter and encourage them into making a mistake …"

But Flintoff was more than just a wind-up merchant; he made himself into the cricketer of his generation through hard work, determination and a hunger to prove the doubters wrong. The stats aren't bad, but they really don't do him justice: England were a more dangerous team when he was on the pitch and he made the team fun to watch.

THE CHIRPING, THE BANTERING, THE SLEDGING

The cricket pitch appears to be a mysterious, silent place when you watch a match from the boundary or amble past on your way to somewhere else, but the reality is that most of the time there is a fairly constant rumble of conversation between the fielders in the moments between the bowlers' deliveries.

There's a purpose to this constant chunter: batters need to keep a high level of concentration if they are going to stay at the crease. They need to focus on the little details in the hope that it can give them a clue about what the bowler has planned and to work out strategies to undermine those plans. They need to be utterly in the moment. So, having some berk from the opposition havering on about the first thing that comes into their head can be slightly off-putting. And in a game like cricket where it's all about fine margins, anything that's slightly off-putting for the batter is good for the fielding team.

While 'it's just banter' is used as an excuse for all kinds of unpleasantness across society, in the case of cricket, it generally is kept gently amusing – otherwise the umpire steps in with a few words of their own.

It can work, though. The absolute classic example comes from England legend Freddie Flintoff (see page 139), who was standing at first slip when Tino Best, batting for the West Indies, came up to the crease. Flintoff decided that Best looked a bit edgy facing the spin of Ashley Giles, and suggested in a jovial manner that Best should, "Mind the windows" – basically suggesting that he, Best, was unlikely to break any windows in the pavilion playing like that. Best was irritated, strode majestically up the wicket to play the ball out of the ground, but unfortunately missed the ball. The wicketkeeper took it, knocked the bails off Best's stumps – and so, off he went back to the pavilion. Presumably not looking round to see the exceedingly smug look on Flintoff's face, although he may well have heard Flintoff's cackle as he walked way.

The thing is, though, sledging can be risky. You've got to be funny with your lines, good at your sport and know who you are talking to. A brave Glamorgan seamer offered Sir Viv Richards (see page 144) some helpful advice to the effect of, "It's red, it's round, you hit it." At which point, Richards smashed the ball beyond the boundary, turned to the bowler and said, "You know what it looks like, now go and find it."

Trying to get under the opposition's skin by winding them up is as old as sport, but the term sledging appears to have emerged in the mid-sixties. There are two versions of the story that do the rounds. In the first, an Australian player is said to have sworn in front of a woman in the crowd and she is said to have reacted as though she'd been hit by a sledgehammer.

The other version of the tale involves an Australian cricketer whose wife was said to be 'carrying on' elsewhere. As he came out to the crease, the fielding team, sensitive to the heavy burden that heartbreak can put on any of us, started singing "When a man loves a woman" by Percy Sledge.

Either way, the word has entered the cricketing lexicon.

• A LITTLE BOOK OF CRICKET •

> "And Glenn McGrath dismissed for two, just 98 runs short of his century."

Richie Benaud, cricketer and commentator, delivers a 13-word masterclass in sledging.

• A LITTLE BOOK OF CRICKET •

★ SIR VIVIAN RICHARDS ★
(WEST INDIES)

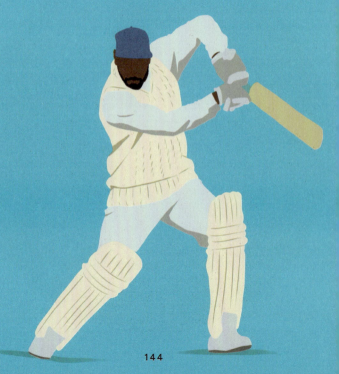

A batter falls, heads back to the dressing room while an expectant hush falls over the stadium. West Indies fans in the stands, despite seeing a wicket fall, start dancing. A pause, and then Viv Richards emerges, bat in hand, and even the opposition fans start sitting forward in their seats anticipating a batting masterclass.

He didn't tend to disappoint, but the frustrating thing for fielding teams was that he made it look so easy, clearing the boundary with languid strokes that didn't waste a watt of energy. Some of his shots looked more like he was opening a round of golf than someone trying to strike a ball that's moving at 90 miles per hour. **Biiiiig** hits taken like he had all the time in the world. The best way to get him out? Keep him off strike and chip away at the players around him.

He made 50 in 12 consecutive matches during 1976, half of them against England, two of which were double centuries and one of which was nearly a triple century. If you look at any batting record possible (and this is cricket so there are many different ways to slice and dice the data), his name will be somewhere in the top 10.

He made it look simple because he had a simple philosophy: "See ball. Hit ball." Sledgers beware.

★ CRICKET PADS ★

The cricket ball is a solid block of cork, string and leather which a modern fast bowler can deliver down the pitch at somewhere between 70 and 90 miles per hour. Combining the density of the ball and the speed at which it can be delivered in the language of advanced physics and spatial mechanics, you are going to know about it if a cricket ball connects with your legs. Pads that offer a bit of protection from the ball are simply common sense.

The problem is that pads can also be used to protect the wicket, to stop the ball from connecting with the stumps and making that horrible plinking noise that batters hate. To get around this, in 1774, the cricket authorities created the leg before wicket (LBW) rule, which gave umpires the right to make a call about whether the ball would have travelled through to the wicket if the batter's leg hadn't got in the way. It's often contentious, but it's probably the least bad option.

The thing is, though, in 1774, the only form of bowling that was technically legal was underarm. It was another three decades or so before some umpires started to give a little bit of latitude to roundarm bowling (see page 47). Overarm wasn't legal under the rules of the game.

If overarm bowling wasn't legal, the risk of injury was significantly lower. So why were batters wearing pads that created the need for an LBW rule?

The answer is the same reason that (probably) Daddy Thomas strode out to the crease with a bat as wide as his wicket in 1771 (see page 26): batters wanted to make it as difficult as possible for the bowler to get them out, and standing in front of the wicket in a big pair of pads was one way to do it. Those years towards the end of the 18th century clearly had a lot of chancers wielding the bat, which is what catalysed the creation of many of the rules of cricket that we know today.

★ WICKETKEEPERS ★

Wicketkeepers are a unique breed. When they are doing their job well, the casual observer doesn't really notice them – they simply lurk behind the wicket, waiting to snatch the ball before it can disappear off in the direction of fine leg or third man and cost the fielding team a run.

That's their job for half the match: spot the bowler about to start their run-up; bob down onto their haunches so they are best positioned to grab the ball; track the ball through the air and then snaffle it before it can do any damage by letting it run away for a bye.

Fast bowlers can't deliver their heavy leather smashes without them, and spin bowlers can't spin their weird webs without them.

Wicketkeeping requires a very specific mindset. Bowlers have their run-up; it's flashy and demands that all eyes are on them. Batters stand alone, noble, chipping away at the score for hour after hour (on a good day), trying to ignore the sledging and taking their split-seconds of divinity when the bad balls come flying at them and they can wield their bats like a knight from days of yore. No one is ever watching the wicketkeeper. They are like statues for most of the game, but when the moment comes, they strike faster than a viper, bringing the ball to the stumps to snatch at the slimmest of opportunities. A good wicketkeeper can be showing sublime skill, but no one is ever really watching.

But the wicketkeeper rarely cares. They are doing their bit for the team, helping bring victory closer with every run saved.

It may look like wicketkeepers don't move, but actually they take up different positions according to who is bowling. With fast bowlers, they retire to a safe distance, not only because a solid mass of leather and horsehair travelling at up to 90 miles per hour can pack a real punch if you are not very careful, but also because if you are further back, you have fractionally more time to react if the ball nicks the bat on the way through.

When the spinners come out to play, though, the wicketkeeper looms closer to the batter and, more importantly, the wicket, their presence reminding the batter of the consequence of deciding to step out of their crease, gallop down the wicket and take a big swing at a shot. "You go right ahead, go for your big moment. But if you miss, I'll be right here."

How close a wicketkeeper stands to the batter is a matter of personal preference; there is no set position. As a result, wicketkeepers can ratchet up the pressure by slowly creeping closer to a higher-order batter's stumps. But they also need to be able to read their teammate with the ball and have a really thick skin – because they are the first person who will be glowered at if the bowler feels that an opportunity has been missed.

The crouching position that the wicketkeeper takes up as the bowler does their thing is actually a relatively new part of the game. Sammy Carter, a wicketkeeper who represented Australia between 1907 and 1921, reasoned that being on your haunches gives you a better chance of reacting to a ball's flight than simply being bent at the waist. From this position, you are already down if the ball is coming through low but can leap for a catch far higher from a crouch than you can when you bend from the waist.

It's also worth noting that teams do not even have to play a wicketkeeper if they decide that they would be better off with an extra fielder. They have to forego the gloves and pads, though, and while it has been tried in professional matches, it's never really caught on.

> "When you are in all day the bat never feels heavy. It is only when you are in and out quickly that it weighs,"

says Colin Cowdrey. Heavy is the hand that carries the bat back to the pavilion.

· A LITTLE BOOK OF CRICKET ·

★ ALAN KNOTT ★
(ENGLAND)

There are household names that transcend the world of cricket and have a wider recognition across society. Alan Knott is not one of those people. He is simply someone who is regularly named as the greatest wicketkeeper/batter ever to grace the sport. The sort of player that most people who know their cricket would put on their list of best cricketers of the last century.

During the 1974/75 Ashes series, he took 15 wicketkeeping dismissals and, almost as importantly, added 364 runs to the England total. In total, he played 95 Tests for England, taking 250 catches and scoring 4,389 runs. He also made five Test hundreds during his career. It could have been six but a pitch invasion forced a match in Pakistan to be abandoned while he stood at the crease with 96 runs under his belt.

Knott played with his collar up long before Eric Cantona, using it to keep the sun off his neck during the long summer days. Even in England.

★ CRICKET AT THE OLYMPICS ★

Despite being 250 years old, cricket has never been more popular worldwide; the men's game is in rude health and the women's game is growing fast. That popularity will be bolstered by cricket's return to the Olympic Games in Los Angeles in 2028, 128 years since the sport last featured.

These days, the Olympic Games are a tightly choreographed affair chock to the gills with corporate sponsors, stewards and *chefs de mission* combining to make sure that everyone gets to the right place at the right time to compete. Things were a little more relaxed back in the early days of the competition's revival at the end of the 19th century.

In the case of cricket, the 1900 Paris Games was supposed to have included a four-way tournament bringing together representatives from Belgium, France, Great Britain and the Netherlands. Unfortunately, the Netherlands couldn't get a full team together and Belgium kind of … seem to have … not sent a team. They probably had a perfectly good reason for their no-show, but they forgot to tell anyone.

As a result, the hastily rearranged final/only match took place between Great Britain and their French hosts. The French team was basically a group of British expats living in Paris, while the British team were a touring club from the West Country. The two teams met at the Vélodrome de Vincennes, thought they all seemed like jolly good fellows and decided to play a 12-a-side match, which Team GB won by a hefty margin. Both teams are said to have been quite surprised to be told that they had actually taken part in the Olympics; they'd thought they were simply taking part in a knockaround as part of a world fair that was taking place at the same time.

Cricket was originally scheduled to be included in the 1904 Olympics in the United States' (US) city of St Louis, but was cancelled due to a lack of entries – and that was it for the next 125 years.

With cricket riding high in the world and starting to get some attention in the US, let's hope that the 2028 Games go without a hitch. It might be an idea to check that Belgium has confirmed they've got their invitation.

★ TAIL-ENDERS ★

After a quarter of a millennium as a formal sport, cricket has become a very specialised business. Sure, you have your all-rounders who can bat a bit and field a bit and bowl a bit if the conditions suit their very specific generalist skill sets, but most people on a cricket team identify as either a batter or a bowler. (Although your wicketkeepers are a bit of a breed apart.)

If you are a bowler, you mostly practise bowling, honing your deliveries to find ways to separate a batter from their wicket with as few runs as possible. That's what you are there to do: send batters back to the changing rooms by bowling tricksy or belligerent balls.

Honing these skills takes time, so there's not usually many hours left in the day to practise batting, but unless the game has gone catastrophically wrong or phenomenally right, bowlers have to bat. So, when it comes down to deciding what order to send the batters out in, captains will tend to send out their specialist batters in the first few slots, and hold off sending the bowlers out to bat until they absolutely have to.

They call it the tail-end because it's where the batting talent is thinnest. Moreover – because cricket is cricket – the tail-end can also wag, which is when the lower-order batters grab a handful of useful runs that can make the difference between winning and the other thing.

> On July 19, 1952, India became the first – and only – international Test team to be dismissed twice in one day. England restricted the visitors to paltry scores of 58 and 82 at Old Trafford to take an unassailable 3-0 lead in the four-match series. However, India did manage to draw the final Test – because it was rained out.

· A LITTLE BOOK OF CRICKET ·

★ STUART BROAD ★
(ENGLAND)

Stuart Broad. 2015. Trent Bridge. Hands to his mouth as he took his eighth Australian wicket for 15 runs. Australia all out for 60. Before lunch. There are few more iconic cricketing moments. The thing about cricket, though, is that this was only 18 months since England had endured an Ashes whitewash, so it was a mighty turnaround.

He wasn't always a bowler; he started out as an opening batter like his father, former England opener Chris Broad, before a growth spurt at 17 gave him the angles to become a devastating fast bowler. It's worth noting that he has the second-most Test ducks, so it could be that his career might not have been so storied if he'd continued on his original trajectory. To be fair, though, he also has the second highest number of runs scored by a number 9 batter, with 169 picked from the pocket of Pakistan at Lord's in 2010. That's how the tail can wag.

Broad retired with a bang in 2023 during the final day of an Ashes series. He scored a six with the final ball he faced with a bat and then took a wicket with the final ball that he bowled. It's hard to think of a better way to say goodbye.

"Not bad for the worst team ever to leave England,"

suggested Mike Gatting after England unexpectedly won the Ashes in Australia in 1986, highlighting the big risk with sledging: it can be used against you if you don't win.